POEMS

By

EDWARD ROWLAND SILL

BOSTON AND NEW YORK
Houghton, Mifflin and Company
The Riverside Press, Cambridge
M DCCC LXXXIX

The Riverside Press, Cambridge:
Electrotyped and Printed by H. O. Houghton & Co.

NOTE.

In presenting this volume of poems to the public it is proper to state briefly the circumstances under which it has been gathered. A year or two ago the publishers, who had noted with interest the poems which Mr. Sill had been contributing to the *Atlantic* and other periodicals, both under his own name and under pseudonyms, invited him to make a collection of his recent poems for publication in a volume. He was in no haste to do this. He was doubtless conscious that his power was a growing one, as indeed the quick succession of poems indicated. At any rate he had that fine sense of poetic art which forbade him to be complacent over his own productions, and he preferred to send fresh poems out, month by month, waiting for the day when a volume should be inevitable.

In the midst of his mental activity, when he was acquiring great flexibility in the use of a variety of literary forms, he died. After his death, so freely, even carelessly, had he let his verses go, that month by month new poems under his familiar signatures appeared in the magazines, as if he went out of the sight of men, singing on his way. It seemed then only just to his memory, and due to literature, which he loved with a generous mind, that the present volume should be gathered. In making choice of its contents it has been thought best to take but five pieces from *The Hermitage and other Poems*, the only volume published by him, and containing his poetic work previous to 1868, the date of its appearance from the house of Leypoldt & Holt. When Mr. Sill bade good-by to his friends in California in 1883, he left with them a small, privately printed volume, bearing the title *The Venus of Milo and other Poems.* A large portion of its contents is included in the present work, which finally contains a selection from the uncollected poems of the last four or five years.

It will be seen by this statement that no attempt has been made to publish the body of Mr. Sill's poetic work, nor even to indicate the quality of his poetry at different periods of his life. Regard has been had to what may properly be considered as his own judgment in such a case, and while a few illustrations are given of the spirit which pervaded his earlier verse and never essentially changed, the main contents are drawn from the poetry which represents his maturity and the period when his technical skill was most highly developed. His own deep respect for his art forbids that his friends should be governed by other considerations than a love and admiration for fine poetry.

Since this volume therefore is addressed not primarily to the friends of Mr. Sill, who would eagerly preserve all that he wrote, but to the larger public that can know his personality only as it is hinted through his verse, a single word may be said regarding his career. He was born in Windsor, Connecticut, in 1841, and graduated at Yale College with the class of 1861. He went to California not long after graduation, and at first engaged in business, but in 1867 returned east with the expectation of entering the ministry, and studied for a few months at the Divinity School of Harvard University. He gave up the purpose, however, married, and occupied himself with literary work, translating Rau's *Mozart*, holding an editorial position on the *New York Evening Mail*, and bringing out his volume of poems.

His peculiar power in stimulating the minds of others drew him into the work of teaching, and he became principal of an academy in Ohio. His California life, however, had given him a strong attachment to the Pacific coast and a sense that his health would be better there, and accordingly, on receiving an invitation to a position in the Oakland High School, he removed to California in 1871, remaining there till 1883. In 1874 he accepted the chair of English Literature in the University of California, and identified himself closely with the literary life which found its expression in magazines and social organization.

Upon his return to the east with the intention of devoting himself more exclusively to literary work, he began that abundant production which has been hinted at, and which, anonymous for the most part, was rapidly giving him facility of execution and drawing attention to the versatility, the insight, the sympathetic power, the inspiring force which had always marked his teaching and bade fair to bring a large and appreciative audience about him. He lived remote from the press of active life, always close to the centre of current intellectual and spiritual movements, in the village of Cuyahoga Falls, Ohio, where he died after a brief illness, February 27, 1887.

NOVEMBER, 1887.

CONTENTS.

Page

The Venus of Milo 1
Field Notes 12
Morning 25
Life 27
Faith 28
Solitude 30
Retrospect 31
Christmas in California 33
Among the Redwoods 38
Opportunity 43
Home 45
Reverie 47
Five Lives 49
Tranquillity 54
Dare You? 56
The Invisible 58
Peace 61
The Fool's Prayer 62
The Deserter 65
The Reformer 66
Desire of Sleep 68

Her Explanation 70
Eve's Daughter 72
Blindfold 74
Recall 76
Strange 78
Wiegenlied 80
An Ancient Error 82
To a Face at a Concert 84
Two Views of it 86
The Links of Chance 88
"Words, Words, Words" 90
The Thrush 93
Carpe Diem 95
Service 96
The Book of Hours 98
The Wonderful Thought 100
Nature and her Child 104
The Foster-Mother 106
Truth at Last 107
"Quem Metui Moritura?" 109
A Morning Thought 111

POEMS

BY

EDWARD ROWLAND SILL

THE VENUS OF MILO.

HERE fell a vision to Praxiteles:
Watching thro' drowsy lids the loitering seas
That lay caressing with white arms of foam
The sleeping marge of his Ionian home,
He saw great Aphrodite standing near,
Knew her, at last, the Beautiful he had sought
With life-long passion, and in love and fear
Into unsullied stone the vision wrought.

Far other was the form that Cnidos gave
To senile Rome, no longer free or brave, —

The Medicean, naked like a slave.
The Cnidians built her shrine
Of creamy ivory fine;
Most costly was the floor
Of scented cedar, and from door
Was looped to carven door
Rich stuff of Tyrian purple, in whose shade
Her glistening shoulders and round limbs outshone,
Milk-white as lilies in a summer moon.
Here honey-hearted Greece to worship came,
And on her altar leaped a turbid flame,
The quickened blood ran dancing to its doom,
And lip sought trembling lip in that rich gloom.

But the island people of Cos, by the salt main
From Persia's touch kept clean,
Chose for their purer shrine amid the seas
That grander vision of Praxiteles.

Long ages after, sunken in the ground
Of sea-girt Melos, wondering shepherds
found
The marred and dinted copy which men
name
Venus of Milo, saved to endless fame.

Before the broken marble, on a day,
There came a worshiper: a slanted ray
Struck in across the dimness of her shrine
And touched her face as to a smile divine;
For it was like the worship of a Greek
At her old altar. Thus I heard him
speak: —

Men call thee Love: is there no holier
name
Than hers, the foam-born, laughter-loving
dame?
Nay, for there is than love no holier name:
All words that pass the lips of mortal men
With inner and with outer meaning shine;
An outer gleam that meets the common
ken,

An inner light that but the few divine.
Thou art the love celestial, seeking still
The soul beneath the form; the serene will;
The wisdom, of whose deeps the sages dream;
The unseen beauty that doth faintly gleam
In stars, and flowers, and waters where they roll;
The unheard music whose faint echoes even
Make whosoever hears a homesick soul
Thereafter, till he follow it to heaven.

Larger than mórtal woman I see thee stand,
With beautiful head bent forward steadily,
As if those earnest eyes could see
Some glorious thing far off, to which thy hand
Invisibly stretched onward seems to be.
From thy white forehead's breadth of calm, the hair

Sweeps lightly, as a cloud in windless air.
Placid thy brows, as that still line at
dawn
Where the dim hills along the sky are
drawn,
When the last stars are drowned in deeps
afar.
Thy quiet mouth — I know not if it smile,
Or if in some wise pity thou wilt weep, —
Little as one may tell, some summer morn,
Whether the dreamy brightness is most
glad,
Or wonderfully sad, —
So bright, so still thy lips serenely sleep ;
So fixedly thine earnest eyes the while,
As clear and steady as the morning star,
Their gaze upon that coming glory keep.

Thy garment's fallen folds
Leave beautiful the fair, round breast
In sacred loveliness ; the bosom deep
Where happy babe might sleep ;
The ample waist no narrowing girdle holds,

Where daughters slim might come to cling
and rest,
Like tendriled vines against the plane-tree
pressed.
Around thy firm, large limbs and steady
feet
The robes slope downward, as the folded
hills
Slope round the mountain's knees, when
shadow fills
The hollow cañons, and the wind is sweet
From russet oat-fields and the ripening
wheat.

From our low world no gods have taken
wing ;
Even now upon our hills the twain are
wandering ;
The Medicean's sly and servile grace,
And the immortal beauty of thy face.
One is the spirit of all short-lived love
And outward, earthly loveliness :
The tremulous rosy morn is her mouth's
smile,

The sky her laughing azure eyes above;
And, waiting for caress,
Lie bare the soft hill-slopes, the while
Her thrilling voice is heard
In song of wind and wave, and every flit-
ting bird.
Not plainly, never quite herself she shows;
Just a swift glance of her illumined smile
Along the landscape goes;
Just a soft hint of singing, to beguile
A man from all his toil;
Some vanished gleam of beckoning arm,
to spoil
A morning's task with longing wild and
vain.
Then if across the parching plain
He seek her, she with passion burns
His heart to fever, and he hears
The west wind's mocking laughter when
he turns,
Shivering in mist of ocean's sullen tears.
It is the Medicean: well I know
The arts her ancient subtlety will show;

The stubble-field she turns to ruddy gold ;
The empty distance she will fold
In purple gauze : the warm glow she has
kissed
Along the chilling mist :
Cheating and cheated love that grows to
hate
And ever deeper loathing, soon or late.

Thou, too, O fairer spirit, walkest here
Upon the lifted hills :
Wherever that still thought within the
breast
The inner beauty of the world hath moved ;
In starlight that the dome of evening fills ;
On endless waters rounding to the west :
For them who thro' that beauty's veil have
loved
The soul of all things beautiful the best.
For lying broad awake, long ere the dawn,
Staring against the dark, the blank of
space
Opens immeasurably, and thy face

Wavers and glimmers there and is with-
drawn.
And many days, when all one's work is
vain,
And life goes stretching on, a waste gray
plain,
With even the short mirage of morning
gone,
No cool breath anywhere, no shadow nigh
Where a weary man might lay him down
and die,
Lo! thou art there before me suddenly,
With shade as if a summer cloud did pass,
And spray of fountains whispering to the
grass.
Oh, save me from the haste and noise and
heat
That spoil life's music sweet:
And from that lesser Aphrodite there —
Even now she stands
Close as I turn, and, O my soul, how fair!
Nay, I will heed not thy white beckoning
hands,

Nor thy soft lips like the curled inner leaf
In a rosebud's breast, kissed languid by
the sun,
Nor eyes like liquid gleams where waters
run.
Yea, thou art beautiful as morn ;
And even as I draw nigh
To scoff, I own the loveliness I scorn.
Farewell, for thou hast lost me : keep thy
train
Of worshipers ; me thou dost lure in vain :
The inner passion, pure as very fire,
Burns to light ash the earthlier desire.

O greater Aphrodite, unto thee
Let me not say farewell. What would
Earth be
Without thy presence? Surely unto me
A life-long weariness, a dull, bad dream.
Abide with me, and let thy calm brows
beam
Fresh hope upon me every amber dawn,
New peace when evening's violet veil is
drawn.

Then, tho' I see along the glooming plain
The Medicean's waving hand again,
And white feet glimmering in the harvest-
field,
I shall not turn, nor yield ;
But as heaven deepens, and the Cross and
Lyre
Lift up their stars beneath the Northern
Crown,
Unto the yearning of the world's desire
I shall be 'ware of answer coming down ;
And something, when my heart the dark-
ness stills,
Shall tell me, without sound or any sight,
That other footsteps are upon the hills ;
Till the dim earth is luminous with the
light
Of the white dawn, from some far-hidden
shore,
That shines upon thy forehead evermore.

FIELD NOTES.*

I.

Y the wild fence-row, all grown up
With tall oats, and the buttercup,
And the seeded grass, and blue
flax-flower,
I fling myself in a nest of green,
Walled about and all unseen,
And lose myself in the quiet hour.
Now and then from the orchard-tree
To the sweet clover at my knee
Hums the crescendo of a bee,
Making the silence seem more still;
Overhead on a maple prong
The least of birds, a jeweled sprite,

* Written for the graduating class of 1882, at Smith College, Northampton, Mass. It is a pleasant custom at that college for each class to send abroad and invite some one to celebrate its entrance into the greater world.

With burnished throat and needle bill,
Wags his head in the golden light,
Till it flashes, and dulls, and flashes bright,
Cheeping his microscopic song.

II.

Far up the hill-farm, where the breeze
Dips its wing in the billowy grain,
Waves go chasing from the plain
On softly undulating seas;
Now near my nest they swerve and turn,
And now go wandering without aim;
Or yonder, where the poppies burn,
Race up the slope in harmless flame.
Sometimes the bold wind sways my walls,
My four green walls of the grass and oats,
But never a slender column falls,
And the blue sky-roof above them floats.
Cool in the glowing sun I feel
On wrist and cheek the sea-breeze steal
From the wholesome ocean brine.
The air is full of the whispering pine,
Surf-sound of an aerial sea;

And the light clashing, near and far,
As of mimic shield and scimitar,
Of the slim Australian tree.

III.

So all that azure day
In the lap of the green world I lay;
And drinking of the sunshine's flood,
Like Sigurd when the dragon's blood
Made the bird-songs understood,
Inward or outward I could hear
A murmuring of music near;
And this is what it seemed to say: —

IV.

Old earth, how beautiful thou art!
Though restless fancy wander wide
And sigh in dreams for spheres more blest,
Save for some trouble, half-confessed,
Some least misgiving, all my heart
With such a world were satisfied.
Had every day such skies of blue,

Were men all wise, and women true,
Might youth as calm as manhood be,
And might calm manhood keep its lore
And still be young — and one thing more,
Old earth were fair enough for me.

Ah, sturdy world, old patient world!
Thou hast seen many times and men;
Heard jibes and curses at thee hurled
From cynic lip and peevish pen.
But give the mother once her due:
Were women wise, and men all true —
And one thing more that may not be,
Old earth were fair enough for me.

V.

If only we were worthier found
Of the stout ball that bears us round!
New wants, new ways, pert plans of change,
New answers to old questions strange;
But to the older questions still
No new replies have come, or will.

New speed to buzz abroad and see
Cities where one needs not to be;
But no new way to dwell at home,
Or there to make great friendships come;
No novel way to seek or find
True hearts and the heroic mind.
Of atom force and chemic stew
Nor Socrates nor Cæsar knew,
But the old ages knew a plan —
The lost art — how to mold a man.

VI.

World, wise old world,
What may man do for thee?
Thou that art greater than all of us,
What wilt thou do to me?
This glossy curve of the tall grass-spear —
Can I make its lustrous green more clear?
This tapering shaft of oat, that knows
To grow erect as the great pine grows,
And to sway in the wind as well as he —
Can I teach it to nod more graciously?
The lark on the mossy rail so nigh,

Wary, but pleased if I keep my place —
Who could give a single grace
To his flute-note sweet and high,
Or help him find his nest hard by?
Can I add to the poppy's gold one bit?
Can I deepen the sky, or soften it?

VII.

Æons ago a rock crashed down
From a mountain's crown,
Where a tempest's tread
Crumbled it from its hold.
Ages dawn and in turn grow old:
The rock lies still and dead.
Flames come and floods come,
Sea rolls this mountain crumb
To a pebble, in its play;
Till at the last man came to be,
And a thousand generations passed away.
Then from the bed of a brook one day
A boy with the heart of a king
Fitted the stone to his shepherd sling,
And a giant fell, and a royal race was
free.

Not out of any cloud or sky
Will thy good come to prayer or cry.
Let the great forces, wise of old,
Have their whole way with thee,
Crumble thy heart from its hold,
Drown thy life in the sea.
And æons hence, some day,
The love thou gavest a child,
The dream in a midnight wild,
The word thou wouldst not say —
Or in a whisper no one dared to hear,
Shall gladden the earth and bring the
golden year.

VIII.

Just now a spark of fire
Flashed from a builder's saw
On the ribs of a roof a mile away.
His has been the better day,
Gone not in dreams, nor even the subtle
desire
Not to desire;
But work is the sober law

He knows well to obey.
It is a poem he fits and fashions well;
And the five chambers are five acts of it:
Hope in one shall dwell,
In another fear will sit;
In the chamber on the east
Shall be the bridal feast;
In the western one
The dead shall lie alone.
So the cycles of life shall fill
The clean, pine-scented rooms where now
he works his will.

IX.

Might one be healed from fevering
thought,
And only look, each night,
On some plain work well wrought,
Or if a man as right and true might be
As a flower or tree!
I would give up all the mind
In the prim city's hoard can find—
House with its scrap-art bedight,

Straitened manners of the street,
Smooth-voiced society —
If so the swiftness of the wind
Might pass into my feet;
If so the sweetness of the wheat
Into my soul might pass,
And the clear courage of the grass;
If the lark caroled in my song;
If one tithe of the faithfulness
Of the bird-mother with her brood
Into my selfish heart might press,
And make me also instinct-good.

X.

Life is a game the soul can play
With fewer pieces than men say.
Only to grow as the grass grows,
Prating not of joys or woes;
To burn as the steady hearth-fire burns;
To shine as the star can shine,
Or only as the mote of dust that turns
Darkling and twinkling in the beam of
light divine;

And for my wisdom — glad to know
Where the sweetest beech-nuts grow,
And to track out the spicy root,
Or peel the musky core of the wild-berry shoot;
And how the russet ground-bird bold
With both slim feet at once will lightly rake the mold;
And why moon-shadows from the swaying limb
Here are sharp and there are dim;
And how the ant his zigzag way can hold
Through the grass that is a grove to him.

'T were good to live one's life alone,
So to share life with many a one:
To keep a thought seven years, and then
Welcome it coming to you
On the way from another's brain and pen,
So to judge if it be true.
Then would the world be fair,
Beautiful as is the past,
Whose beauty we can see at last,
Since self no more is there.

XI.

I will be glad to be and do,
And glad of all good men that live,
For they are woof of nature too;
Glad of the poets every one,
Pure Longfellow, great Emerson,
And all that Shakspeare's world can give.
When the road is dust, and the grass dries,
Then will I gaze on the deep skies;
And if Dame Nature frown in cloud,
Well, mother — then my heart shall say —
You cannot so drive me away;
I will still exult aloud,
Companioned of the good hard ground,
Whereon stout hearts of every clime,
In the battles of all time,
Foothold and couch have found.

XII.

Joy to the laughing troop
That from the threshold starts,

Led on by courage and immortal hope,
And with the morning in their hearts.
They to the disappointed earth shall give
The lives we meant to live,
Beautiful, free, and strong;
The light we almost had
Shall make them glad;
The words we waited long
Shall run in music from their voice and
song.
Unto our world hope's daily oracles
From their lips shall be brought;
And in our lives love's hourly miracles
By them be wrought.
Their merry task shall be
To make the house all fine and sweet
Its new inhabitants to greet,
The wondrous dawning century.

XIII.

And now the close of this fair day was
come;
The bay grew duskier on its purple floor,

And the long curve of foam
Drew its white net along a dimmer shore.
Through the fading saffron light,
Through the deepening shade of even,
The round earth rolled into the summer night,
And watched the kindling of the stars in heaven.

MORNING.

ENTERED once, at break of day,
A chapel, lichen-stained and gray,
Where a congregation dozed and heard
An old monk read from a written Word.
No light through the window-panes could pass,
For shutters were closed on the rich stained-glass;
And in a gloom like the nether night
The monk read on by a taper's light.
Ghostly with shadows, that shrank and grew
As the dim light flared, were aisle and pew;
And the congregation that dozed around,
Listened without a stir or sound —

Save one, who rose with wistful face,
And shifted a shutter from its place.
Then light flashed in like a flashing gem —
For dawn had come unknown to them —
And a slender beam, like a lance of gold,
Shot to the crimson curtain-fold,
Over the bended head of him
Who pored and pored by the taper dim;
And it kindled over his wrinkled brow
Such words — "The law which was till
now;"
And I wondered that, under that morning
ray,
When night and shadow were scattered
away,
The monk should bow his locks of white
By a taper's feebly flickering light —
Should pore, and pore, and never seem
To notice the golden morning-beam.

LIFE.

FORENOON and afternoon and night, — Forenoon,
And afternoon, and night, — Forenoon, and — what!
The empty song repeats itself. No more?
Yea, that is Life: make this forenoon sublime,
This afternoon a psalm, this night a prayer,
And Time is conquered, and thy crown is won.

FAITH.

THE tree-top, high above the barren field,
Rising beyond the night's gray folds of mist,
Rests stirless where the upper air is sealed
To perfect silence, by the faint moon kiss'd.
But the low branches, drooping to the ground,
Sway to and fro, as sways funereal plume,
While from their restless depths low whispers sound —
"We fear, we fear the darkness and the gloom;
Dim forms beneath us pass and re-appear,
And mournful tongues are menacing us here."

Then from the topmost bough falls calm reply —
"Hush, hush! I see the coming of the morn;
Swiftly the silent Night is passing by,
And in her bosom rosy Dawn is borne.
'T is but your own dim shadows that ye see,
'T is but your own low moans that trouble ye."

So Life stands, with a twilight world around;
Faith turned serenely to the steadfast sky,
Still answering the heart that sweeps the ground,
Sobbing in fear, and tossing restlessly —
"Hush, hush! The Dawn breaks o'er the Eastern sea,
'T is but thine own dim shadow troubling thee."

SOLITUDE.

LL alone — alone,
Calm, as on a kingly throne,
Take thy place in the crowded land,
Self-centred in free self-command.
Let thy manhood leave behind
The narrow ways of the lesser mind :
What to thee are its little cares,
The feeble love or the spite it bears ?
Let the noisy crowd go by:
In thy lonely watch on high,
Far from the chattering tongues of men,
Sitting above their call or ken,
Free from links of manner and form
Thou shalt learn of the wingèd storm —
God shall speak to thee out of the sky.

RETROSPECT.

NOT all which we have been
Do we remain,
Nor on the dial-hearts of men
Do the years mark themselves in vain;
But every cloud that in our sky hath passed,
Some gloom or glory hath upon us cast;
And there have fallen from us, as we traveled,
Many a burden of an ancient pain —
Many a tangled chord hath been unraveled,
Never to bind our foolish heart again.
Old loves have left us lingeringly and slow,
As melts away the distant strain of low
Sweet music — waking us from troubled dreams,
Lulling to holier ones — that dies afar
On the deep night, as if by silver beams

Claspt to the trembling breast of some
charmed star.
And we have stood and watched, all wist-
fully,
While fluttering hopes have died out of
our lives,
As one who follows with a straining eye
A bird that far, far-off fades in the sky,
A little rocking speck — now lost; and
still he strives
A moment to recover it — in vain;
Then slowly turns back to his work again.
But loves and hopes have left us in their
place,
Thank God! a gentle grace,
A patience, a belief in His good time,
Worth more than all earth's joys to which
we climb.

CHRISTMAS IN CALIFORNIA.

CAN this be Christmas — sweet as May,
With drowsy sun, and dreamy air,
And new grass pointing out the way
For flowers to follow, everywhere?

Has Time grown sleepy at his post,
And let the exiled Summer back,
Or is it her regretful ghost,
Or witchcraft of the almanac?

While wandering breaths of mignonette
In at the open window come,
I send my thoughts afar, and let
Them paint your Christmas Day at home.

Glitter of ice, and glint of frost,
  And sparkles in the crusted snow;
And hark! the dancing sleigh-bells, tost
  The faster as they fainter grow.

The creaking footsteps hurry past;
  The quick breath dims the frosty air;
And down the crisp road slipping fast
  Their laughing loads the cutters bear.

Penciled against the cold white sky,
  Above the curling eaves of snow,
The thin blue smoke lifts lingeringly,
  As loth to leave the mirth below.

For at the door a merry din
  Is heard, with stamp of feathery feet,
And chattering girls come storming in,
  To toast them at the roaring grate.

And then from muff and pocket peer,
  And many a warm and scented nook,

Mysterious little bundles queer,
  That, rustling, tempt the curious look.

Now broad upon the southern walls
  The mellowed sun's great smile appears,
And tips the rough-ringed icicles
  With sparks, that grow to glittering tears.

Then, as the darkening day goes by,
  The wind gets gustier without,
And leaden streaks are on the sky,
  And whirls of snow are all about.

Soon firelight shadows, merry crew,
  Along the darkling walls will leap
And clap their hands, as if they knew
  A thousand things too good to keep.

Sweet eyes with home's contentment filled,
  As in the smouldering coals they peer,
Haply some wondering pictures build
  Of how I keep my Christmas here.

Before me, on the wide, warm bay,
  A million azure ripples run ;
Round me the sprouting palm-shoots lay
  Their shining lances to the sun.

With glossy leaves that poise or swing,
  The callas their white cups unfold,
And faintest chimes of odor ring
  From silver bells with tongues of gold.

A languor of deliciousness
  Fills all the sea-enchanted clime ;
And in the blue heavens meet, and kiss,
  The loitering clouds of summer-time.

This fragrance of the mountain balm
  From spicy Lebanon might be ;
Beneath such sunshine's amber calm
  Slumbered the waves of Galilee.

O wondrous gift, in goodness given,
  Each hour anew our eyes to greet,

An earth so fair — so close to Heaven,
  'T was trodden by the Master's feet.

And we — what bring we in return?
  Only these broken lives, and lift
Them up to meet His pitying scorn,
  As some poor child its foolish gift:

As some poor child on Christmas Day
  Its broken toy in love might bring;
You could not break its heart and say
  You cared not for the worthless thing?

Ah, word of trust, His child! That child
  Who brought to earth the life divine,
Tells me the Father's pity mild
  Scorns not even such a gift as mine.

I am His creature, and His air
  I breathe, where'er my feet may stand;
The angels' song rings everywhere,
  And all the earth is Holy Land.

AMONG THE REDWOODS.

FAREWELL to such a world! Too long I press
The crowded pavement with unwilling feet.
Pity makes pride, and hate breeds hatefulness,
And both are poisons. In the forest, sweet
The shade, the peace! Immensity, that seems
To drown the human life of doubts and dreams.

Far off the massive portals of the wood,
Buttressed with shadow, misty-blue, serene,
Waited my coming. Speedily I stood
Where the dun wall rose roofed in plumy green.

Dare one go in? — Glance backward! Dusk as night
Each column, fringed with sprays of amber light.

Let me, along this fallen bole, at rest,
Turn to the cool, dim roof my glowing face.
Delicious dark on weary eyelids prest!
Enormous solitude of silent space,
But for a low and thunderous ocean sound,
Too far to hear, felt thrilling through the ground.

No stir nor call the sacred hush profanes;
Save when from some bare tree-top, far on high,
Fierce disputations of the clamorous cranes
Fall muffled, as from out the upper sky.
So still, one dreads to wake the dreaming air,
Breaks a twig softly, moves the foot with care.

The hollow dome is green with empty
shade,
Struck through with slanted shafts of
afternoon ;
Aloft, a little rift of blue is made,
Where slips a ghost that last night was
the moon ;
Beside its pearl a sea-cloud stays its
wing,
Beneath a tilted hawk is balancing.

The heart feels not in every time and
mood
What is around it. Dull as any stone
I lay ; then, like a darkening dream, the
wood
Grew Karnak's temple, where I breathed
alone
In the awed air strange incense, and up-
rose
Dim, monstrous columns in their dread re-
pose.

The mind not always sees; but if there
shine
A bit of fern-lace bending over moss,
A silky glint that rides a spider-line,
On a trefoil two shadow-spears that
cross,
Three grasses that toss up their nodding
heads,
With spring and curve like clustered foun-
tain-threads, —

Suddenly, through side windows of the
eye,
Deep solitudes, where never souls have
met;
Vast spaces, forest corridors that lie
In a mysterious world, unpeopled yet.
Because the outward eye elsewhere was
caught,
The awfulness and wonder come unsought.

If death be but resolving back again
Into the world's deep soul, this is a kind

Of quiet, happy death, untouched by pain
Or sharp reluctance. For I feel my mind
Is interfused with all I hear and see;
As much a part of All as cloud or tree.

Listen! A deep and solemn wind on high;
The shafts of shining dust shift to and fro;
The columned trees sway imperceptibly,
And creak as mighty masts when trade-winds blow.
The cloudy sails are set; the earth-ship swings
Along the sea of space to grander things.

OPPORTUNITY.

THIS I beheld, or dreamed it in a dream: —
There spread a cloud of dust along a plain;
And underneath the cloud, or in it, raged
A furious battle, and men yelled, and swords
Shocked upon swords and shields. A prince's banner
Wavered, then staggered backward, hemmed by foes.
A craven hung along the battle's edge,
And thought, "Had I a sword of keener steel —
That blue blade that the king's son bears, — but this
Blunt thing — !" he snapt and flung it from his hand,

And lowering crept away and left the field.
Then came the king's son, wounded, sore
bestead,
And weaponless, and saw the broken
sword,
Hilt-buried in the dry and trodden sand,
And ran and snatched it, and with battle-
shout
Lifted afresh he hewed his enemy down,
And saved a great cause that heroic day.

HOME.

THERE lies a little city in the hills;
White are its roofs, dim is each dwelling's door,
And peace with perfect rest its bosom fills.

There the pure mist, the pity of the sea,
Comes as a white, soft hand, and reaches o'er
And touches its still face most tenderly.

Unstirred and calm, amid our shifting years,
Lo! where it lies, far from the clash and roar,
With quiet distance blurred, as if thro' tears.

O heart, that prayest so for God to send
Some loving messenger to go before
And lead the way to where thy longings end,

Be sure, be very sure, that soon will come
His kindest angel, and through that still door
Into the Infinite love will lead thee home.

REVERIE.

WHETHER 't was in that dome of evening sky,
So hollow where the few great stars were bright,
Or something in the cricket's lonely cry,
Or, farther off, where swelled upon the night
The surf-beat of the symphony's delight,
Then died in crumbling cadences away —
A dream of Schubert's soul, too sweet to stay :

Whether from these, or secret spell within, —
It seemed an empty waste of endless sea,
Where the waves mourned for what had never been,

Where the wind sought for what could
never be :
Then all was still, in vast expectancy
Of powers that waited but some mystic
sign
To touch the dead world to a life divine.

Me, too, it filled — that breathless, blind
desire ;
And every motion of the oars of thought
Thrilled all the deep in flashes — sparks
of fire
In meshes of the darkling ripples caught,
Swiftly rekindled, and then quenched to
naught ;
And the dark held me ; wish and will
were none :
A soul unformed and void, silent, alone,
And brooded over by the Infinite One.

FIVE LIVES.

FIVE mites of monads dwelt in a round drop
That twinkled on a leaf by a pool in the sun.
To the naked eye they lived invisible;
Specks, for a world of whom the empty shell
Of a mustard-seed had been a hollow sky.

One was a meditative monad, called a sage;
And, shrinking all his mind within, he thought:
"Tradition, handed down for hours and hours,
Tells that our globe, this quivering crystal world,
Is slowly dying. What if, seconds hence,

When I am very old, yon shimmering dome
Come drawing down and down, till all things end?"
Then with a weazen smirk he proudly felt
No other mote of God had ever gained
Such giant grasp of universal truth.

One was a transcendental monad; thin
And long and slim in the mind; and thus he mused:
"Oh, vast, unfathomable monad-souls!
Made in the image"—a hoarse frog croaks from the pool—
"Hark! 't was some god, voicing his glorious thought
In thunder music! Yea, we hear their voice,
And we may guess their minds from ours, their work.
Some taste they have like ours, some tendency

To wriggle about, and munch a trace of
scum."
He floated up on a pin-point bubble of gas
That burst, pricked by the air, and he was
gone.

One was a barren-minded monad, called
A positivist; and he knew positively:
"There is no world beyond this certain
drop.
Prove me another! Let the dreamers
dream
Of their faint gleams, and noises from
without,
And higher and lower; life is life enough."
Then swaggering half a hair's breadth,
hungrily
He seized upon an atom of bug, and fed.

One was a tattered monad, called a
poet;
And with shrill voice ecstatic thus he
sang:

"Oh, the little female monad's lips!
Oh, the little female monad's eyes!
Ah, the little, little, female, female monad!"

The last was a strong-minded monadess,
Who dashed amid the infusoria,
Danced high and low, and wildly spun and dove
Till the dizzy others held their breath to see.

But while they led their wondrous little lives
Æonian moments had gone wheeling by.
The burning drop had shrunk with fearful speed;
A glistening film — 't was gone; the leaf was dry.
The little ghost of an inaudible squeak
Was lost to the frog that goggled from his stone;

Who, at the huge, slow tread of a thoughtful ox
Coming to drink, stirred sideways fatly, plunged,
Launched backward twice, and all the pool was still.

TRANQUILLITY.

WEARY, and marred with care and pain
And bruising days, the human brain
Draws wounded inward, — it might be
Some delicate creature of the sea,
That, shuddering, shrinks its lucent dome,
And coils its azure tendrils home,
And folds its filmy curtains tight
At jarring contact, e'er so light;
But let it float away all free,
And feel the buoyant, supple sea
Among its tinted streamers swell,
Again it spreads its gauzy wings,
And, waving its wan fringes, swings
With rhythmic pulse its crystal bell.

So let the mind, with care o'erwrought,
Float down the tranquil tides of thought:

Calm visions of unending years
Beyond this little moment's fears ;
Of boundless regions far from where
The girdle of the azure air
Binds to the earth the prisoned mind.
Set free the fancy, till it find
Beyond our world a vaster place
To thrill and vibrate out through space,—
As some auroral banner streams
Up through the night in pulsing gleams,
And floats and flashes o'er our dreams ;
There let the whirling planet fall
Down — down, till but a glimmering ball,
A misty star : and dwindled so,
There is no room for care, or woe,
Or wish, apart from that one Will
That doth the worlds with music fill.

DARE YOU?

OUBTING Thomas and loving
John,
Behind the others walking on: —

"Tell me now, John, dare you be
One of the minority?
To be lonely in your thought,
Never visited nor sought,
Shunned with secret shrug, to go
Thro' the world esteemed its foe;
To be singled out and hissed,
Pointed at as one unblessed,
Warred against in whispers faint,
Lest the children catch a taint;
To bear off your titles well, —
Heretic and infidel?
If you dare, come now with me,
Fearless, confident, and free."

" Thomas, do you dare to be
Of the great majority?
To be only, as the rest,
With Heaven's common comforts blessed;
To accept, in humble part,
Truth that shines on every heart;
Never to be set on high,
Where the envious curses fly;
Never name or fame to find,
Still outstripped in soul and mind;
To be hid, unless to God,
As one grass-blade in the sod,
Underfoot with millions trod?
If you dare, come with us be
Lost in love's great unity.

THE INVISIBLE.

F there is naught but what we see,
What is the wide world worth to me?
But is there naught save what we see?
A thousand things on every hand
My sense is numb to understand:
I know we eddy round the sun;
When has it dizzied any one?
I know the round worlds draw from far,
Through hollow systems, star to star;
But who has e'er upon a strand
Of those great cables laid his hand?
What reaches up from room to room
Of chambered earth, through glare or gloom,
Through molten flood and fiery blast,
And binds our hurrying feet so fast?
'T is the earth-mother's love, that well

Will hold the motes that round her dwell:
Through granite hills you feel it stir
As lightly as through gossamer:
Its grasp unseen by mortal eyes,
Its grain no lens can analyze.

If there is naught but what we see,
The friend I loved is lost to me:
He fell asleep; who dares to say
His spirit is so far away?
Who knows what wings are round about?
These thoughts — who proves but from without
They still are whispered? Who can think
They rise from morning's food and drink!
These thoughts that stream on like the sea,
And darkly beat incessantly
The feet of some great hope, and break,
And only broken glimmers make,
Nor ever climb the shore, to lie
And calmly mirror the far sky,
And image forth in tranquil deeps
The secret that its silence keeps.

Because he never comes, and stands
And stretches out to me both hands,
Because he never leans before
The gate, when I set wide the door
At morning, nor is ever found
Just at my side when I turn round,
Half thinking I shall meet his eyes,
From watching the broad moon-globe
rise, —
For all this, shall I homage pay
To Death, grow cold of heart, and say:
" He perished, and has ceased to be;
Another comes, but never he " ?
Nay, by our wondrous being, nay!
Although his face I never see
Through all the infinite To Be,
I know he lives and cares for me.

PEACE.

IS not in seeking,
'T is not in endless striving,
Thy quest is found:
Be still and listen;
Be still and drink the quiet
Of all around.

Not for thy crying,
Not for thy loud beseeching,
Will peace draw near:
Rest with palms folded;
Rest with thine eyelids fallen —
Lo! peace is here.

THE FOOL'S PRAYER.

THE royal feast was done; the King
Sought some new sport to banish care,
And to his jester cried: "Sir Fool,
Kneel now, and make for us a prayer!"

The jester doffed his cap and bells,
And stood the mocking court before;
They could not see the bitter smile
Behind the painted grin he wore.

He bowed his head, and bent his knee
Upon the monarch's silken stool;
His pleading voice arose: "O Lord,
Be merciful to me, a fool!

"No pity, Lord, could change the heart
From red with wrong to white as wool;

The rod must heal the sin : but Lord,
  Be merciful to me, a fool !

" 'T is not by guilt the onward sweep
  Of truth and right, O Lord, we stay ;
'T is by our follies that so long
  We hold the earth from heaven away.

" These clumsy feet, still in the mire,
  Go crushing blossoms without end ;
These hard, well-meaning hands we thrust
  Among the heart-strings of a friend.

" The ill-timed truth we might have kept —
  Who knows how sharp it pierced and
    stung ?
The word we had not sense to say —
  Who knows how grandly it had rung ?

" Our faults no tenderness should ask,
  The chastening stripes must cleanse
    them all ;
But for our blunders — oh, in shame
  Before the eyes of heaven we fall.

"Earth bears no balsam for mistakes;
Men crown the knave, and scourge the tool
That did his will; but Thou, O Lord,
Be merciful to me, a fool!"

The room was hushed; in silence rose
The King, and sought his gardens cool,
And walked apart, and murmured low,
"Be merciful to me, a fool!"

THE DESERTER.

BLINDEST and most frantic
prayer,
Clutching at a senseless boon,
His that begs, in mad despair,
Death to come ; — he comes so soon !

Like a reveler that strains
Lip and throat to drink it up —
The last ruby that remains,
One red droplet in the cup.

Like a child that, sullen, mute,
Sulking spurns, with chin on breast,
Of the Tree of Life a fruit,
His gift of whom he is the guest.

Outcast on the thither shore,
Open scorn to him shall give
Souls that heavier burdens bore : —
" See the wretch that dared not live ! "

THE REFORMER.

BEFORE the monstrous wrong he sets him down —
One man against a stone-walled city of sin.
For centuries those walls have been a-building;
Smooth porphyry, they slope and coldly glass
The flying storm and wheeling sun. No chink,
No crevice lets the thinnest arrow in.
He fights alone, and from the cloudy ramparts
A thousand evil faces gibe and jeer him.
Let him lie down and die: what is the right,
And where is justice, in a world like this?

But by and by, earth shakes herself, impatient;
And down, in one great roar of ruin, crash
Watch-tower and citadel and battlements.
When the red dust has cleared, the lonely soldier
Stands with strange thoughts beneath the friendly stars.

DESIRE OF SLEEP.

IT is not death I mean,
Nor even forgetfulness,
But healthful human sleep,
Dreamless, and still, and deep,
Where I would hide and glean
Some heavenly balm to bless.

I would not die ; I long
To live, to see my days
Bud once again, and bloom,
And make amidst them room
For thoughts like birds of song,
Out-winging happy ways.

I would not even forget :
Only, a little while —
Just now — I cannot bear
Remembrance with despair ;

The years are coming yet
  When I shall look, and smile.

Not now — oh, not to-night!
  Too clear on midnight's deep
Come voice and hand and touch;
The heart aches overmuch —
  Hush sounds! shut out the light!
  A little I *must* sleep.

HER EXPLANATION.

SO you have wondered at me, — guessed in vain
What the real woman is you know so well?
I am a lost illusion. Some strange spell
Once made your friend there, with his fine disdain
Of fact, conceive me perfect. He would fain
(But could not) see me always, as befell
His dream to see me, plucking asphodel,
In saffron robes, on some celestial plain.
All that I was he marred and flung away
In quest of what I was not, could not be, —
Lilith, or Helen, or Antigone.

Still he may search; but I have had my
day,
And now the Past is all the part for me
That this world's empty stage has left to
play.

EVE'S DAUGHTER.

WAITED in the little sunny
room :
The cool breeze waved the window-lace, at play,
The white rose on the porch was all in bloom,
And out upon the bay
I watched the wheeling sea-birds go and come.

" Such an old friend, — she would not make me stay
While she bound up her hair." I turned, and lo,
Danaë in her shower ! and fit to slay
All a man's hoarded prudence at a blow :
Gold hair, that streamed away
As round some nymph a sunlit fountain's flow.

"She would not make me wait!"—but well I know
She took a good half-hour to loose and lay
Those locks in dazzling disarrangement so!

BLINDFOLD.

WHAT do we know of the world, as
we grow so old and wise?
Do the years, that still the heart-
beats, quicken the drowsy eyes?
At twenty we thought we knew it, — the
world there, at our feet;
We thought we had found its bitter, we
knew we had found its sweet.
Now at forty and fifty, what do we make
of the world?
There in her sand she crouches, the
Sphinx with her gray wings furled.
Soul of a man I know not; who knoweth,
can foretell,
And what can I read of fate, even of self
I have learned so well?
Heart of a woman I know not: how
should I hope to know,

I that am foiled by a flower, or the stars
of the silent snow ;
I that have never guessed the mind of the
bright-eyed bird,
Whom even the dull rocks cheat, and the
whirlwind's awful word ?
Let me loosen the fillet of clay from the
shut and darkened lid,
For life is a blindfold game, and the Voice
from view is hid.
I face him as best I can, still groping,
here and there,
For the hand that has touched me lightly,
the lips that have said, " Declare ! "
Well, I declare him my friend, — the
friend of the whole sad race ;
And oh, that the game were over, and I
might see his face !
But 't is much, though I grope in blind-
ness, the Voice that is hid from
view
May be heard, may be even loved, in a
dream that may come true.

RECALL.

"LOVE me, or I am slain!" I cried, and meant
Bitterly true each word. Nights, morns, slipped by,
Moons, circling suns, yet still alive am I;
But shame to me, if my best time be spent

On this perverse, blind passion! Are we sent
Upon a planet just to mate and die,
A man no more than some pale butterfly
That yields his day to nature's sole intent?

Or is my life but Marguerite's ox-eyed flower,
That I should stand and pluck and fling away,
One after one, the petal of each hour,

Like a love-dreamy girl, and only say,
" Loves me," and " loves me not," and
" loves me " ? Nay !
Let the man's mind awake to manhood's
power.

STRANGE.

HE died at night. Next day they
came
To weep and praise him : sudden
fame
These suddenly warm comrades gave.
They called him pure, they called him
brave ;
One praised his heart, and one his brain ;
All said, You 'd seek his like in vain, —
Gentle, and strong, and good : none saw
In all his character a flaw.

At noon he wakened from his trance,
Mended, was well ! They looked askance ;
Took his hand coldly ; loved him not,
Though they had wept him ; quite forgot
His virtues ; lent an easy ear
To slanderous tongues ; professed a fear

He was not what he seemed to be;
Thanked God they were not such as he;
Gave to his hunger stones for bread;
And made him, living, wish him dead.

WIEGENLIED.

E still and sleep, my soul!
Now gentle-footed Night
In softly shadowed stole,
Holds all the day from sight.

Why shouldst thou lie and stare
Against the dark, and toss,
And live again thy care,
Thine agony and loss?

'T was given thee to live,
And thou hast lived it all;
Let that suffice, nor give
One thought what may befall.

Thou hast no need to wake,
Thou art no sentinel;
Love all the care will take,
And Wisdom watcheth well.

Weep not, think not, but rest!
The stars in silence roll;
On the world's mother-breast,
Be still and sleep, my soul!

AN ANCIENT ERROR.

He that has, and a little tiny wit, —
With a heigh, ho, the wind and the rain.

LEAR.

THE "sobbing wind," the "weeping rain," —
'T is time to give the lie
To these old superstitions twain,
That poets sing and sigh.

Taste the sweet drops, — no tang of brine;
Feel them, — they do not burn;
The daisy-buds, whereon they shine,
Laugh, and to blossoms turn.

There is no natural grief or sin;
'T is we have flung the pall,
And brought the sound of sorrow in.
Pan is not dead at all.

The merry Pan! his blithesome look
  Twinkles through sun and rain;
By ivied rock and rippled brook
  He pipes his jocund strain.

If winds have wailed and skies wept tears,
  To poet's vision dim,
'T was that his own sobs filled his ears,
  His weeping blinded him.

'T is laughing breeze and singing shower,
  As ever heart could need;
And who with "heigh" and "ho" must
      lower
  Hath "tiny wit" indeed.

TO A FACE AT A CONCERT.

WHEN the low music makes a dusk of sound
About us, and the viol or far-off horn
Swells out above it like a wind forlorn,
That wanders seeking something never found,
What phantom in your brain, on what dim ground,
Traces its shadowy lines? What vision, born
Of unfulfillment, fades in mere self-scorn,
Or grows, from that still twilight stealing round?
When the lids droop and the hands lie unstrung,

Dare one divine your dream, while the chords weave
Their cloudy woof from key to key, and die, —
Is it one fate that, since the world was young,
Has followed man, and makes him half believe
The voice of instruments a human cry?

TWO VIEWS OF IT.

WORLD, O glorious world, good-by!"
Time but to think it — one wild cry
Unuttered, a heart-wrung farewell
To sky and wood and flashing stream,
All gathered in a last swift gleam,
As the crag crumbled, and he fell.

But lo! the thing was wonderful!
After the echoing crash, a lull:
The great fir on the slope below
Had spread its mighty mother-arm,
And caught him, springing like a bow
Of steel, and lowered him safe from harm.

'T was but an instant's dark and daze:
Then, as he felt each limb was sound,

And slowly from the swooning haze
The dizzy trees stood still that whirled,
And the familiar sky and ground,
There grew with them across his brain
A dull regret : " So, world, dark world,
You are come back again ! "

THE LINKS OF CHANCE.

HOLDING apoise in air
My twice-dipped pen, — for some tense thread of thought
Had snapped, — mine ears were half aware
Of passing wheels; eyes saw, but mind saw not,
My sun-shot linden. Suddenly, as I stare,
Two shifting visions grow and fade unsought: —

Noon-blaze: the broken shade
Of ruins strown. Two Tartar lovers sit:
She gazing on the ground, face turned, afraid;

And he, at her. Silence is all his wit.
She stoops, picks up a pebble of green jade
To toss: they watch its flight, unheeding it.

Ages have rolled away;
And round the stone, by chance, if chance there be,
Sparse toil has caught; a seed, wind-lodged one day,
Grown grass; shrubs sprung; at last a tufted tree:
Lo! over its snake root yon conquering Bey
Trips backward, fighting — and half Asia free!

"WORDS, WORDS, WORDS."

(TO ONE WHO FLOUTED THEM AS VAIN.)

I.

AM I not weary of them as your heart
Or ever Hamlet's was? — the empty ones,
Mere breath of passing air, mere hollow tones
That idle winds to broken reeds impart.

Have they not cursed my life? — sounds I mistook
For sacred verities, — love, faith, delight,
And the sweet tales that women tell at night,
When darkness hides the falsehood of the look.

I was the one of all Ulysses' crew
(What time he stopped their ears) that leaped and fled
Unto the sirens, for the honey-dew

Of their dear songs. The poets me have fed
With the same poisoned fruit. And even you, —
Did you not pluck them for me in days dead?

II.

Nay, they do bear a blessing and a power, —
Great words and true, that bridge from soul to soul
The awful cloud-depths that betwixt us roll.
I will not have them so blasphemed. This hour,

This little hour of life, this lean to-day, —
What were it worth but for those mighty
dreams
That sweep from down the past on sound-
ing streams
Of such high-thoughted words as poets
say?

What, but for Shakespeare's and for Ho-
mer's lay,
And bards whose sacred names all lips
repeat?
Words, — only words; yet, save for tongue
and pen

Of those great givers of them unto men,
And burdens they still bear of grave or
sweet,
This world were but for beasts, a darkling
den.

THE THRUSH.

THE thrush sings high on the top-
most bough, —
Low, louder, low again ; and now
He has changed his tree, — you know not
how,
For you saw no flitting wing.

All the notes of the forest-throng,
Flute, reed, and string, are in his song;
Never a fear knows he, nor wrong,
Nor a doubt of anything.

Small room for care in that soft breast ;
All weather that comes is to him the best,
While he sees his mate close on her nest,
And the woods are full of spring.

He has lost his last year's love, I know, —
He, too, — but 't is little he keeps of woe;
For a bird forgets in a year, and so
  No wonder the thrush can sing.

CARPE DIEM.

HOW the dull thought smites me dumb,
"It will come!" and "It will come!"
But to-day I am not dead;
Life in hand and foot and head
Leads me on its wondrous ways.
'T is in such poor, common days,
Made of morning, noon, and night,
Golden truth has leaped to light,
Potent messages have sped,
Torches flashed with running rays,
World-runes started on their flight.

Let it come, when come it must;
But To-Day from out the dust
Blooms and brightens like a flower,
Fair with love, and faith, and power.
Pluck it with unclouded will,
From the great tree Igdrasil.

SERVICE.

FRET not that the day is gone,
And thy task is still undone.
'T was not thine, it seems, at all:
Near to thee it chanced to fall,
Close enough to stir thy brain,
And to vex thy heart in vain.
Somewhere, in a nook forlorn,
Yesterday a babe was born:
He shall do thy waiting task;
All thy questions he shall ask,
And the answers will be given,
Whispered lightly out of heaven.
His shall be no stumbling feet,
Falling where they should be fleet;
He shall hold no broken clue;
Friends shall unto him be true;
Men shall love him; falsehood's aim
Shall not shatter his good name.

Day shall nerve his arm with light,
Slumber soothe him all the night;
Summer's peace and winter's storm
Help him all his will perform.
'T is enough of joy for thee
His high service to foresee.

THE BOOK OF HOURS.

S one who reads a tale writ in a tongue
He only partly knows, — runs over it
And follows but the story, losing wit
And charm, and half the subtle links among
The haps and harms that the book's folk beset, —
So do we with our life. Night comes, and morn :
I know that one has died and one is born ;
That this by love and that by hate is met.
But all the grace and glory of it fail
To touch me, and the meanings they enfold.

The Spirit of the World hath told the tale,
And tells it : and 't is very wise and old.
But o'er the page there is a mist and veil :
I do not know the tongue in which 't is told.

THE WONDERFUL THOUGHT.

T comes upon me in the woods,
Of all the days, this day in May :
When wind and rain can never think
Whose turn 't is now to have its way.

It finds me as I lie along,
Blinking up through the swaying trees,
Half wondering if a man who reads
" Blue sky " in books *that* color sees, —

So fathomless and pure : as if
All loveliest azure things have gone
To heaven that way, — the flowers, the sea, —
And left their color there alone.

Hark ! leaning on each other's arms,
The pines are whispering in the breeze,

Whispering, — then hushing, half in awe
Their legends of primeval seas.

The wild things of the wood come out,
And stir or hide, as wild things will,
Like thoughts that may not be pursued,
But come if one is calm and still.

Deep hemlocks down the gorge shut in
Their caves with hollow shadow filled,
Where little feathered anchorites
Behind a sunlit lattice build.

And glimmering through that lace of boughs,
Dancing, while they hang darker still,
Along the restful river shines
The restless light's incessant thrill:

As in some sober, silent soul,
Whose life appears a tranquil stream,
Through some unguarded rift you catch
The wildest wishes, all agleam.

But to my thought — so wonderful!
  I know if once 't were told, all men
Would feel it warm at heart, and life
  Be more than it had ever been.

'T would make these flowerless woods
      laugh out
  With every garden-color bright,
Where only, now, the dogwood hangs
  Its scattered cloud of ghostly white.

Those birds would hold no more aloof: —
  How know they I am here, so well?
'Tis yon woodpecker's warning note;
  He is their seer and sentinel.

They use him, but his faithfulness
  Perchance in human fashion pay, —
Laugh in their feathers at his voice,
  And ridicule his stumbling way.

That far-off flute-note — hours in vain
  I 've followed it, so shy and fleet;

But if I found him, well I know
  His song would seem not half so sweet.

The swift, soft creatures, — how I wish
  They 'd trust me, and come perch upon
My shoulders! Do they guess that then
  Their charm would be forever gone?

But still I prate of sight and sound;
  Ah, well, 't is always so in rhyme;
The idle fancies find a voice,
  The wise thought waits — another time.

NATURE AND HER CHILD.

AS some poor child whose soul is
  windowless,
Having not hearing, speech, nor
  sight, sits lone
In her dark, silent life, till cometh one
With a most patient heart, who tries to
  guess

Some hidden way to help her helplessness,
And, yearning for that spirit shut in stone,
A crystal that has never seen the sun,
Smooths now the hair, and now the hand
  will press,

Or gives a key to touch, then letters
  raised,
Its symbol; then an apple, or a ring,
And again letters, — so, all blind and
  dumb,

We wait; the kindly smiles of summer
come,
And soft winds touch our cheek, and
thrushes sing;
The world-heart yearns, but we stand dull
and dazed.

THE FOSTER-MOTHER.

AS some poor Indian woman
  A captive child receives,
And warms it in her bosom,
  And o'er its weeping grieves;

And comforts it with kisses,
  And strives to understand
Its eager, lonely babble,
  Fondling the little hand, —

So Earth, our foster-mother,
  Yearns for us, with her great
Wild heart, and croons in murmurs
  Low, inarticulate.

She knows we are white captives,
  Her dusky race above,
But the deep, childless bosom
  Throbs with its brooding love.

TRUTH AT LAST.

DOES a man ever give up hope, I wonder, —
Face the grim fact, seeing it clear as day?
When Bennen saw the snow slip, heard its thunder
Low, louder, roaring round him, felt the speed
Grow swifter as the avalanche hurled downward,
Did he for just one heart-throb — did he indeed
Know with all certainty, as they swept onward,
There was the end, where the crag dropped away?
Or did he think, even till they plunged and fell,

Some miracle would stop them? Nay, they tell
That he turned round, face forward, calm and pale,
Stretching his arms out toward his native vale
As if in mute, unspeakable farewell,
And so went down. — 'T is something, if at last,
Though only for a flash, a man may see
Clear-eyed the future as he sees the past,
From doubt, or fear, or hope's illusion free.

"QUEM METUI MORITURA?"

ÆNEID, IV. 604.

WHAT need have I to fear — so soon to die?
Let me work on, not watch and wait in dread:
What will it matter, when that I am dead,
That they bore hate or love who near me lie?
'T is but a lifetime, and the end is nigh
At best or worst. Let me lift up my head
And firmly, as with inner courage, tread
Mine own appointed way, on mandates high.
Pain could but bring, from all its evil store,
The close of pain: hate's venom could but kill;

Repulse, defeat, desertion, could no more.
Let me have lived my life, not cowered until
The unhindered and unhastened hour was here.
So soon — what is there in the world to fear?

A MORNING THOUGHT.

WHAT if some morning, when the stars were paling,
And the dawn whitened, and the East was clear,
Strange peace and rest fell on me from the presence
Of a benignant Spirit standing near:

And I should tell him, as he stood beside me,
"This is our Earth — most friendly Earth, and fair;
Daily its sea and shore through sun and shadow
Faithful it turns, robed in its azure air:

"There is blest living here, loving and serving,
And quest of truth, and serene friendships dear;

But stay not, Spirit! Earth has one destroyer —
His name is Death: flee, lest he find thee here!"

And what if then, while the still morning brightened,
And freshened in the elm the Summer's breath,
Should gravely smile on me the gentle angel
And take my hand and say, "My name is Death."

www.ingramcontent.com/pod-product-compliance
Lightning Source LLC
LaVergne TN
LVHW021423110826
845150LV00007B/2059

* 9 7 8 1 4 2 5 5 0 8 2 9 6 *